GUN CONTROL IN AMERICA
Should Guns Be Banned In America?

BY

RYAN DANIELS

Congratulations!!!

You have just downloaded a copy of "Gun Control in America: Should Guns Be Banned in America?".

This book will give you an idea of what to do if you were in a situation with a shooter in a school or just out in the public somewhere.

I really hope you enjoy reading this book and if i may ask you for a favor, can you kindly leave a review after reading the book. Thank You!!

Table of Contents

Introduction 1

Chapter 1: Guns for Safety...5

Chapter 2: Do You Carry An Unloaded Handgun? 9

Chapter 3: Gun Control an Issue for Our Times 13

Chapter 4: Putting it altogether...19

Chapter 5: The 2nd and 10th Amendments...23

Chapter 6: California's Gun Control Laws and Legislation 35

Chapter 7: Gun Control Explained..39

Chapter 8: Guns crime In the USA 43

Chapter 9: Six Things to Teach About School Rampage Shootings........... 47

Chapter 10: Teachers and Guns in Schools 51

Chapter 11: Ways thought to Manage Gun shooting in schools 55

Chapter 12: Lock-Down Procedure and Related Insurance....................57

Chapter 13: What You Can Do- School Shootings 61

Chapter 14: My Independent Thought on Guns in Schools 63

Conclusion 67

INTRODUCTION

The U.S. collectively mourned the deaths of children and teachers in the Newtown, Connecticut, shootings and recently Marjory Stoneman Douglas High School in Parkland, Florida. United in grief and empathy for those directly affected, social media sites lit up like a Times Square New Year with prayers, tears, grief, charity, and love, directed to those involved. Children, parents, and sympathetic citizens signed cards, drew pictures, raised money, and did their very best to put smiles back on the survivors.

It took only a matter of hours before the shouts on each side of the gun debate became screams, and I noticed people lining up, similar to the recent political election positions in both passion and division, about how to fix this mess we've made.

Governments from Virginia and Tennessee and probably many other states had promises from governors and senators that proposals to arm teachers and administrations would appear on agendas immediately after the holiday break. The NRA announced that allowing, perhaps even requiring, some teachers and administrators to carry a weapon as the "best way to protect children from gun violence."

The social workers, not to be out shouted, also presented their case, calling for counseling and screening procedures that allow more intensive interaction with kids on edge. Many argue that engaging more guns will do nothing to stop the violence, especially if one decides to use an entirely different method of destruction, such as a truck filled with explosives. Others argue that schools need to be protected and prepared, openly declaring to anyone interested in starting up a gunfight that fire will be met with fire.

Parents are worried. Teachers are angry. Legislators are trying to appease their constituents. Judges are trying to interpret a Constitution written for a civilization grown way beyond the seams of that colonial garment. The civilized world is appalled. What is the answer? Will installing marshals in schools, or requiring certain teachers, staff, and administrators to carry guns, save lives? Or will it take more?

It is a very serious, very critical matter, protecting our schools. Whether it requires teachers and administrators to be trained and required to carry guns is an entirely different matter. The discussion has a lot to dovetail into the heart of the matter, including mental health treatment, counseling, respect, education, and hope, along with the courage to do the right thing. Where it will all lead depends on our input as citizens. Now might be a very good time to get involved and let legislators know what we are thinking, and let our students know we are doing more than wringing our hands and wrangling with our opposition. Kids need our help, and the government needs our input. Let's find a way to give it.

CHAPTER 1

GUNS FOR SAFETY

Finding statistics for how effective guns are at reducing crime is very difficult. We can point to the fact that on average 22,000 people a year are killed from accident or suicide with guns – and that is far higher than the rate of legal gun murders in self-defense. But a robbery you stopped isn't going to be part of any statistic and you won't even know if someone avoided assaulting you on the grounds you might have a gun.

Many gun advocates claim that not only are guns not dangerous but they create lower rates of crime and provide a good deterrent against crime.

Many elements of gun control wouldn't impact this.

Safe gun storage, ensuring gun owners could safely use guns, cooling off periods, and thorough mental health checks don't stop you getting a gun. If the aim of guns is self-defense and overthrowing tyrants, wouldn't train in how to use a gun help with this? Other nations, as listed above, have real tests or permits and civilians still own guns in huge numbers.

Defending yourself and your families are considered one of the most important reasons to ensure guns are not taken away. Overall, just as gun ownership doesn't seem to have an enormous impact on how much gun violence there is, there doesn't seem to be a global trend for countries with higher gun ownership rates having lower rates of crime. However, that just means culture overrides the impact of guns.

It could still be the case that guns reduce rates of home invasions, burglaries, assaults, and muggings. Are guns going to be more effective than simply having a good lock on your door and avoiding isolated locations where muggings are likely? It's hard to tell, and if crime statistics are only low because people need to live in fortresses, it's not exactly a good situation to be in.

If requiring gun training would severely reduce the number of gun owners you would still have to worry about the owners that would have been able to get them without a test. Even banning assault rifles and high capacity guns would not stop you being able to use a gun in self-defense or as a crime deterrent.

Nevertheless, if we did have good evidence that guns reduced crime and made things safer, ensuring that guns were easily available to anyone that could safely handle one would be important.

Self Defense

Legally your right to defend yourself with a gun is not clear. In many states, you aren't allowed to shoot someone simply because they are robbing your stuff and you can't blow someone away just because they are threatening you. You do need to feel you are actually in danger for your life and even then the law might not protect you in some states.

CHAPTER 2

DO YOU CARRY AN UNLOADED HANDGUN?

With all the discussion going on in the media about gun control and because of my occupation as a law enforcement officer, I often get corralled into conversations about gun ownership. I had one such conversation with my friend Beth recently.

She was very excited to tell me that she had purchased her first handgun for self-defense. I was a bit surprised because Beth has three children under the age of 6 and is, by nature, rather timid. I decided to ask her more questions about how she carried and used it, and if having a firearm around her children caused her any concern.

Beth told me she didn't worry about the kids because she didn't load the gun when she carried it on her person. "I keep a few bullets in a container in my glove box, in case I need them." She then added, "I figure if someone comes up to us, I'll just take the gun out and hopefully scare them with it."

While her answer made me cringe, I didn't judge her, because I knew that she was putting the safety of her children at the forefront. I also knew that her self-defense strategy was more common than I cared to think about.

While the children would be safe from any gunfire from Beth's gun, she was not only still at risk, but by carrying an unloaded gun, she was placing herself at greater risk than if she had nothing at all.

The purpose of a gun should never be to 'scare' anyone. It should be used only as a last result. If you brandish it, then you should be prepared to follow through and use it. If you pull a firearm on a bad guy and they have a gun as well, which will no doubt be loaded, they are more likely to use it against you. Additionally, if you brandished yours first, and they shoot, there is always the possibility that they will use self-defense as their legal defense.

Attacks rarely come with a warning. I try to imagine a scenario where an attacker can be put on hold while you load your weapon. "Excuse me a minute, Mr. Bad Guy. I just need to get something in my glove box." It's just not practical.

I gave Beth my advice as tactfully and non-judgmentally as possible. Her safety concerned me than I was about whether or not she would still like me. I also suggested that she replace the handgun with a stun gun.

No, it may not have the same stopping power that a .40 caliber bullet would, but she could keep it fully charged... locked and loaded, without having to worry about the safety of her children.

Knowing her temperament, I also knew she would be more likely to use a nonlethal form of self-defense than she would a gun, even to protect herself.

If you have considered getting a handgun for your protection, then make sure you understand how to use it safely, practice regularly with it, and please keep it loaded. You also need to be aware of the moral and legal implications of using lethal force.

While I am all for the right of law-abiding, mentally stable citizens to be able to own firearms, I am a bigger proponent for the use of nonlethal force.

Ultimately, your goal should be to stay safe, not to kill someone.

CHAPTER 3

GUN CONTROL AN ISSUE FOR OUR TIMES

The recent media footage of the destruction of innocent, young lives re-ignites the gun reform debate again, and what we as a community can do to prevent another tragedy. The outpourings of grief and horror are becoming all too frequent in our society. What has gone wrong? Why do human beings feel the need to express their anger and disappointment with their lives by resorting to such extreme violence? The ramifications of easily accessible firearms are like opening a Pandora's Box. If the owner is mentally stable, then the likelihood of the devastating consequences such as those we have been witness to in Newtown Connecticut, is small. However, if someone who is unstable, and who is unlikely to take responsibility for their actions, has easy access to high powered firearms, the likely consequences can be more readily predicted.

In Australia, the Port Arthur massacre was the turning point for gun reform laws. Ownership of weapons is now subject to far stricter controls and legislation. The United States of America is a different matter with a population of 314,947,000 making it a far more difficult and complex issue to grapple with. The massive gun control lobby has far-reaching influences across the States. In their Constitution 'the right to bear arms' acts like a mantra too much of the population. President Trump will have an enormous battle on his hands if he attempts to change the Constitution and enforce stricter gun laws. Americans, supported by the National Rifle Association and its 4.3 million members continue to display a fierce, almost obsessive affinity for weapons.

Why is it that the pro-gun lobby and anti-gun lobby have so much difficulty in coming together logically and sensibly to discuss this issue? It is highly emotive, and naturally enough, emotions run high. Gun owners believe it is their right to be able to have weapons for recreational purposes and to defend themselves, if and when the situation occurs. The remaining populace believes that this should not be the case, because of the unknown factor of a person's mental faculties, and the ease with which these dangerous weapons, in the hands of the wrong person, can inflict such damage and bloodshed. Somewhere, in the midst of all this, is another cross-section of the community who are largely ambivalent.

Canada on the other hand has gun laws that are far more stringent than the United States. At least two references are required for any potential gun owner, and their knowledge and understanding of that person has to have been apparent for a minimum of three years. Confirmation that a new owner is not likely to be a menace to society is also a prerequisite, along with a thorough background check. A minimum waiting period of 28 days is standard before any firearm is registered and the transaction approved. In contrast to these rules and regulations, the State of Connecticut, which was the latest example of a firearm tragedy, has only a 14 day waiting period before completing a firearm purchase. Under Federal Law, any individual who is considered mentally defective, convicted of a felony, or misdemeanors will be refused gun ownership.

If the United States of America were successful in changing their Constitution, the probability of these horrendous violent acts would hopefully be diminished considerably. If gun owners had to register each weapon, have them safely stored in an appropriate gun cabinet, and were only allowed for farmers and those who need them in the course of their employment or are members of recognized sporting shooters clubs; society would be very different. Everybody is accountable for their actions, and unfortunately, these types of atrocities happen when the person using their weapon does not feel any social responsibility, is unable to deal with their anger and frustration in a non-violent manner, or is mentally unstable.

The voting power of the massive U.S. gun lobby is huge. The President will be under enormous pressure to start making gun law reforms, not just express condolences and shock at what has transpired during the most recent firearm massacre, at Newtown, Connecticut. One of the facets of gun law reform would be to police and ban any form of private advertising and sale of weapons. This will be hard to enforce, but there may be ways and means of putting strategies in place to prevent just anybody and everybody from being able to purchase guns without testing their credibility as a responsible owner. The power to make constructive changes to gun law reform is now in the hands of the President and those who believe that enough is enough!

Stand-your-ground laws aren't strictly about gun control, but in places where you can carry a gun in public or to have free access to them in the home, it is a question about guns. In short, the question is about whether or not you should be allowed to defend yourself with lethal force when you are, or feel you are, threatened.

In many states as long as you have a gun with you in a legal way (meaning you can't have a concealed illegal weapon), you can kill someone in self-defense if you need to. Importantly with this law, you do not need to retreat or to look for non-lethal methods to defend yourself. Without laws such as this, you can still be held responsible if it seems your attempt to defend yourself went beyond what was reasonable given the circumstances. In other words in states without these laws, you could still get in trouble if you shot someone dead after they attacked you.

This concerns guns because defending yourself with lethal force is a much bigger issue if civilians are carrying guns. Also without the ability to lethally defend your life with a gun it's questionable whether guns are practical tools of self-defense.

Those opposed usually argue that it encourages people to shoot each other, it puts justice in the hands of untrained civilians, and with it, there is a lot of room for abuse. You could feasibly goad someone into attacking you and then shoot them – though you would have to kill them in one shot for that to work successfully.

Those in favor say these laws are fundamental to self-defense and they will help to lower crime rates.

CHAPTER 4

PUTTING IT ALTOGETHER

Before we start quoting the constitutional law or declaring the USA is in a state of emergency full of gun-toting maniacs let's see what checks there are for the average person looking to buy and own a gun legally.

If someone goes to buy a gun from a licensed seller, they will need to pass a background check that ensures they don't have a history of mental illness or criminal wrong-doings. In most states, they don't need a permit or need to wait out cooling off period. If they buy a handgun, it must come with a basic safety storage device (such as a trigger lock).

If they want to buy a high-caliber Title 2 gun, it needs to be registered, and they need to pay a $200 tax on it. In general, though the government holds records, and it is not always recorded that you even tried to get a background check.

They can't have a gun shipped directly to their door, but if they buy privately, they don't need to pass a background check in many states. They can own as many guns as they want though and there aren't many laws about how they need to be stored at home.

If they want to conceal or open carry a gun they will usually need to file for registration, and they can't usually conceal carry anything other than a handgun, and it can't be a handgun adapted to look like something other than a handgun. To carry across state lines, the gun needs to be safely stored in the vehicle.

In general getting a gun legally is relatively simple and quick, there is not that much information on the record of you doing so, safety is up to the individual, and getting the ability to carry it around with you everywhere is fairly simple in most states. Most central to the debate though is the fact you can get around background checks in many states, and there are few restrictions on assault rifles.

You probably noticed one of the big issues here is the difference between federal and state law. In some states such as California gun laws are already quite strict, but in others such as Alabama, there are few regulations beyond what is federally required. Arguing across the entire country can make things confusing –especially since you can't truly compare statistics between states that vary in crime and wealth.

When President Trump is talking about gun control, he is talking about what he calls 'common sense' gun laws. This is taken to mean ensuring there are thorough background checks, licenses in place when selling any guns, full mental health screening when it comes to buying guns and the banning of unnecessarily powerful rifles and guns (usually the assault rifle).

The huge number of possibilities when it comes to gun control makes the debate difficult for many, and it's made more difficult when different parties are arguing against each other about different things. If one party merely wants background checks for guns, then they're not trying to take your guns away. If a person thinks guns are fundamental to having a free country they aren't going to care that people can get hold of them with ease.

CHAPTER 5

THE 2ND AND 10TH AMENDMENTS

It is extremely troubling to note the inappropriate, or just basically wrong, responses of, supposedly, knowledgeable federal and State government officers to ignorant U.S. citizens who act and speak irresponsibly as though they know nothing at all about the U.S. Constitution and its timely purpose in today's 21st Century society. In the wake of mass murders committed by mentally deranged human beings using firearms, there are presently individuals, and groups of individuals, around the republic clamoring for the federal government to create laws, decrees, and orders that will alter and diminish the right of the sane, reasonable, and responsible citizens of the USA to keep and bear arms, meaning firearms under the 2nd Amendment of the Bill of Rights. My friend, attorney Mark Levin, was totally correct when he recently stated that "no one, it seems, wants to discuss the U.S. Constitution today in its correct context meaningfully." That's exactly what I want to do in this chapter, regarding the sacred right to keep and bear arms.

The honored Framers of the 1787 Constitutional Convention, including James Madison, Benjamin Franklin, John Jay, and John Adams, with Thomas Jefferson advising from France, were not devoid of wisdom when they crafted, and the State legislatures ratified, the Bill of Rights, which were the first ten amendments to the U.S. Constitution. A majority of that Convention refused even to discuss a constitution without assurance that a Bill of Rights would be included. Nine of the twenty-six provisions stated within the Bill of Rights was crafted from the articles of the great Magna Carta, or the Great Charter, drafted in 1215 by the Archbishop of Canterbury and signed by King John of England in June of that year. Of course, bows, arrows, spears, knives, and swords were the only weapons of war available at that time to the common Englishman, but as times changed, weapons, or arms, changed and improved in their lethal effectiveness. The U.S. Constitution was, as James Madison exclaimed in his "Federalist 44," to specifically limit the federal government in its power and to empower the rights of the State governments, or the People. This principle of federalism was delineated very specifically in the 10th Amendment of the Bill of Rights, which very few of the literate citizens of the USA currently understand and comprehend. The 10th Amendment states, "The powers not delegated to the United States by the Constitution, nor prohibited by it to the States, are reserved to the States respectively, or to the people." This 10th Amendment has been called by some the exclusive 10th Amendment police power of the States, or the People because it provides for an open-ended opportunity for the States to craft their laws to properly police and protect their People by the specific prohibitions concerning their powers within the Constitution. In other words, the States have the power to legislate any State laws to benefit their people which are not specifically denied to them by the U.S. Constitution. For instance, a State cannot conduct foreign affairs with a foreign power, such as Mexico or Japan. This is a power specifically delegated to the federal government's Executive branch in the Constitution. States have the power to create their own money as legal tender for payment of debts, providing that that money is in the form of gold or silver coins. This is what might be called a joint power with the federal government, since Article 1, Section 8 specifically states that the federal government has the only power to "print" federal paper money for use throughout the USA as legal tender for purchases and debts. The State of Utah is one of the States that has created its gold currency through a State legislated law.

Now, what about the 2nd Amendment regarding the 10th Amendment police power of the States? The 2nd Amendment simply affirms that "A well-regulated Militia, being necessary to the security of a free State, the right of the people to keep and bear arms shall not be infringed." This constraint applies to both the federal government and the State governments; yet, if considered properly, a very interesting application proceeds from it. The federal government "cannot" diminish to any degree, or infringe upon, the right of the people to keep and bear arms, which it has illegally done by passing legislation to impose gun registration laws upon the States. Nonetheless, the States have the open-ended power to expand those laws, as does the federal government, extending greater rights to the People to keep and bear arms. For instance, the States have the right to allow their People to carry handguns openly, and to pass laws setting age restrictions for purchasing, owning, and carrying handguns; but for a State, or a federal district, to pass laws flatly denying its citizens the right to purchase, possess, and carry firearms is a blatant infringement of the 2nd Amendment. In other words, the federal government cannot denigrate, to any degree, by legislation, the right of the People to keep and bear arms. It can, however, promote the welfare of the States by promoting, or encouraging, the States to pass laws that will provide the greatest safety for the People through the purchasing, keeping, and bearing firearms.

At this juncture in this chapter, the practicable and utilitarian example of the State of Texas' use of their 10th Amendment police power has an important application to all of the fifty American States. The legendary Texas Rangers were a force to be reckoned-with during an early period of prevailing lawlessness on a Republic of Texas' frontier, and as a newly annexed State; and the Rangers continue to be a formidable means of effective law enforcement in the 21st Century. The old expression still applies as a basic truism in Texas, "one riot, one Texas Ranger," where the audacious, yet prudent, power and authority of a good stern person wielding a handgun for the sake of justice, law, and order is confirmed in the minds of the lawless. The States, all of the States, have an open-ended power to train and arm anyone it so chooses to protect their people. The federal government, on the other hand, has no Constitutional power, whatsoever, to place armed federal police, or military personnel, in the cities and towns of the States to enforce State or federal laws. When people from other States drive into a Texas town and see a sign in bold letters at the city-limits that says, "Beware, murderers, bank robbers, thieves, and rapists... Our school teachers, store-owners, and most of our citizens are armed and know how to use their weapons very effectively. So, don't mess with us," it goes a long way in driving-home the reality that the people of that town are very serious about protecting their own. And they have a God-given right to do so. Any sign along a Texas highway boldly saying, "Don't Mess With Texas," goes way beyond the warning and penalties for littering. On the other hand, if you every sees a sign in a city or town saying, "Beware, the FBI is on the job here," you are witnessing an expression of federal intimidation through the unconstitutional use of federal power. Federal law enforcement, the FBI, U.S. Marshalls, the Secret Service, etc. can never legally impose itself on State, county, and local law enforcement; that is, unless a federal crime has been committed, or if invited by a State to assist in an investigation.

So, when the crowds of ignorant and disingenuous people, both U.S. Citizens, legally visiting aliens, and illegal aliens, petition in front of the White House, the federal Capitol Building, and the U.S.

Supreme Court for federal Executive orders, federal legislations, and U.S. Supreme Court activism to create unconstitutional laws restricting the right of the People, under the 2nd Amendment, to keep and bear arms, the reasonable and prudent People of the republic, and the news media in support of those reasonable citizens, should immediately decry such unconstitutional demonstrations and vociferously proclaim the Constitutional right of the States to police and protect their citizens under the 2nd Amendment and the 10th Amendment of the Bill of Rights. All State school systems, by State legislation of laws, should very discriminately choose responsible and caring teachers, and guards, to be trained and armed with handguns to carry, and use when necessary, while on-duty in their schools, in order to protect the lives of the students and unarmed faculty from deranged murderers who steal onto their campuses. There is no doubt that, if responsible guards and teacher(s), both men and women, had been trained, armed, and present on the campuses, in the classrooms and hallways where mass-murders have been committed in the schools around the USA, the probability would have been very high that the deranged assailants would have been quickly neutralized before they would have done any lethal harm.

There are many other reasons for caring and responsible men and women to be effectively trained to carry and use handguns, as there are many good reasons for keeping rifles and handguns in the homes of law-abiding families, many more reasons than not keeping and bearing firearms. One very important truth should always be remembered when considering the importance of keeping and bearing firearms. If the good and decent citizens of the republic are restricted by unconstitutional government action from keeping and bearing arms in defense of their families, friends, communities, and the common law, the only people who will end-up possessing handguns, rifles, and shotguns will be those sinister people with criminal intents and purposes who will use the tens of millions of black-marketed firearms available to them for murderous and illegitimate purposes. It is good also to remember that the militia, as defined by the 2nd Amendment and by James Madison in his "Federalist 46," are the men, women, and adolescents of mature age, the People of the USA, who keep and bear arms in the republic.

Now we arrive at probably the most provocative element of the awful misuse of the 10th Amendment police power by the States. This has been the copycat effect of the States following federal action in imposing, over the decades of the 20th Century, unnecessary exorbitant taxation upon the People, and then woefully misusing it. This unlawful effect is inexorably prevalent in the 21st Century and has been so since 1913, when the sordid 16th Amendment was, supposedly, legally ratified by the State legislatures. For reasons contrary to the astute wisdom of the Framers, the federal government saw pragmatic purpose in making what was unconstitutional in 1912 apparently constitutional in 1913, that being un-apportioned taxation in the form of a federal income tax. As the proverbial apple does not, in most cases, fall far from its parent tree, the parent example of the federal government imposing un-apportioned taxation upon the States gave most of the States an incentive over time to do the same horrible thing to its citizens. By the mid-20th Century, most the States had pragmatically legislated State income taxes upon their electorates, and by 1960, the States were taxing their hardworking People 2,000 percent more than King George III had unlawfully taxed the American colonists in 1775. Of course, King George III had taxed the colonists without their representation in the British Parliament, while the State legislatures pompously claimed that they were producing necessary taxation through a process based upon the proper representation of their citizens. This unsubstantiated claim of representation and support of the State electorates was, and still is, without merit, and was founded totally upon a false perception of what small wealthy minorities of overtaxed State electorates have claimed is being done with the exorbitant tax revenue obtained by forced collection. As it still stands since 1913, the popular desire of the great majority of the State electorates is the abrogation of all state and federal income tax through the repeal of the 16th Amendment.

As the "security" of the "blessings of liberty and natural law" was the purpose end-result of the establishment of the American Constitution, as proclaimed in its often forgotten Preamble, the 10th Amendment police power was predicated upon the protection of those liberties and freedoms by the States. Moreover, the honorable Framer James Madison wrote extensively upon the sacredness of the money, the income, earned by citizens of the American republic, and the evil of a federal government effort to tax it. He fully delineated, in the "Federalist Papers" the reason why federal and State government should always seek to limit, instead of expanding, it's taxing authority upon the People.

While the States maddeningly pursue the unmitigated taxation of their People, their misuse of that exorbitant tax money in not providing for the protection of their people is, yet, another salient issue. Most of the State, county, and municipal governments use great amounts of tax money to maintain their law enforcement agencies. The standard expression used by most governors, county commissioners, mayors, and city managers, "let the police deal with violent crime that exists," and to a reasonable degree this is wise counsel, as far as the investigation, apprehension, and arrest of criminal perpetrators are concerned, after the commission of violent crimes. Yet, the 2nd Amendment was set in place as a preventive deterrent to crime, and as a protective means for the People, or the States, in order to ensure their safety and liberty; since the State, county, and municipal police cannot, in most cases, be on the scene all of the time to prevent all crimes (murders, burglaries, rapes) from happening.

While most of the States is, by far, following the unreasonable example of the federal government of legislating unnecessary and improper laws, the creation of their superfluous laws and executive agencies for their execution illustrate what those State governments are not doing; that is, fully protecting their People. Since they, and they alone, have the Constitutional 10th Amendment power and responsibility to protect and serve the People, the passage of such laws by the State legislatures is essential. Most of the States are greatly over-taxing their citizens and then using that ill-gotten revenue for socialistic purposes while neglecting the need to protect their People. Those arcane 21st Century State, and federal, politicians who still stupidly insist that the honored Framers were, either, unable or unwilling to craft a meaningful U.S. Constitution for all the ages to come are doing great disservice to the republic through their blatant propaganda, which is sad evidence of their own ignorance of relevant history.

While, for example, the federal government is to, alone, provide for the common national defense by maintenance and use of the U.S. Military, the States, every one of them, are to, alone, provide for the maintenance of law enforcement and social order with them, through use of their open-ended police powers. In the same way that the Framers gave the States total control over the education of their People, civil rights, agriculture, abortion, and every other matter not specifically delegated to the federal government by the Constitution, those wise men (who were assuredly counseled and advised by their sagacious wives) essentially instructed the States through the explicit letter of the U.S. Constitution to do "whatever" was necessary, within their power, to protect their People from criminals and their criminally destructive ways. Nonetheless, as the States continue to flippantly and carelessly tax their people and build unnecessary government bureaucracies, funding them exorbitantly, the great majority of them are grossly deficient in producing legislation to adequately protect their citizens in an age of unbounded criminal conspiracies and social and political turmoil. The criminal upending of morality and the desecration of natural law by deliberate political design brings with it heinous consequences and their pernicious effect on the American family, the education of the youth of the States, and on the ultimate mission of the States to protect and perpetuate liberty.

Therefore, in the pure interest of preserving and protecting human life and for the perpetuation of liberty, the State governments should immediately cease their obeisance to, and deferential respect for, unconstitutional federal government Legislative, Executive, and Judicial actions and properly use the power bestowed by the U.S. Constitution 10th Amendment upon them, or the People. There is nothing more grand and godly than the preservation of human life and liberty through the proper exercise and use of law; for, as the great John Adams so vehemently stated, "We are a nation of laws, and not of men."

CHAPTER 6

CALIFORNIA'S GUN CONTROL LAWS AND LEGISLATION

California has the stringent laws controlling the use of guns in the country with approximately 950 firearm laws currently in effect. Supporters of stricter gun laws argue that these laws are necessary to curb crime and enhance safety, while critics of gun control argue that the laws infringe upon the Constitutional right to bear arms afforded to all citizens by the Second Amendment and that safety is reduced because citizens are less able to use firearms to protect themselves. Because there are very few federal firearms laws, individual states have been left to "control the sale, ownership, and usage of firearms ammunition and firearms." As a result, state laws vary significantly from state-to-state.

In 2012 alone, no fewer than six bills have been introduced in California that addresses existing gun laws or creates new gun laws. These bills include:

Senate Bill 610 - Concealed Handgun Permit Application (in effect since January 2012)

Senate Bill 819 - Transfer of Background Check Fees (in effect since January 2012)

Assembly Bill 144 - Unloaded Handgun Open Carry Ban (in effect since January 2012)

Assembly Bill 809 - Long Gun Registration Law (effective in 2014)

Assembly Bill 1527 - Long Gun Open Carry Ban (pending)

Senate Bill 427 - Ammunition Registration (vetoed)

Senate Bill 610 states that Gun owners are not required to obtain liability insurance before getting a permit to carry a concealed weapon. The law also standardizes the application process and does not require an applicant to pay for training courses before obtaining a permit. This was the only recent legislation that was applauded by groups who urge less restrictive gun laws.

Senate Bill 819 allows the Department of Justice to access the Dealer Record of Sales (DROS) funds to pay for the enforcement of certain gun possession laws. Originally, DROS funds were used only to pay for the administrative costs of obtaining background checks. Critics of this law argue that there will be insufficient DROS funds to fund enforcement.

Gun control advocates supported both Assembly Bill 144 and 809. AB 144 prohibits a person from openly carrying an unloaded handgun in most public places, and is already effective; and AB 809 will become effective on January 1, 2014, and requires the registration of all newly purchased rifles and shotguns. Currently, no state need registration of rifles or shotguns, and only new residents of California are required to register handguns within 60 days. Failure to register a handgun is a misdemeanor; however, law enforcement typically will not charge gun owners who comply with the registration law after the 60 days.

In the wake of the recent gun crimes in Arizona and Colorado, Assembly Bill 1527 was recently passed in California and is now awaiting the governor to approve or veto. The bill would prohibit the open carry of long guns, which includes rifles and shotguns. Critics of AB 1527 argue that this is unconstitutional, while supporters argue that this is merely a necessary expansion of AB 144, which now outlaws the carry of open unloaded handguns. Supporters argue that the sight of rifles and shotguns can be frightening and should be prohibited in most public places.

Governor Jerry Brown, who is a gun-owner, vetoed Senate Bill 427, which would have allowed police to obtain records of sales from retailers of ammunition, required retailers to notify the police if they intended to sell ammunition; and prohibited the online and mail order purchase of certain calibers of ammunition. Critics of SB 427 argued that many of the calibers of ammunition that were identified in the law are popular among hunters, and would have an impact on sales.

In general, groups that advocate for gun laws argue that strict gun laws help reduce violence, particularly domestic violence. Advocates point out that states with strict gun laws have lower incidences of suicides and crimes of passion that result in homicide. In 2010, 8,775 out of almost 13,000 murders were committed with firearms. Opponents of gun laws, however, argue that the right to bear arms must not be infringed upon, and that law-abiding citizens do not need restrictions; while non law-abiding gun owners will not be deterred from criminal activity regardless of gun laws. A 2010 survey estimates that approximately 300 million firearms are owned by civilians in the United States, which is 50% of all guns in the world. It is figured that there are 88 guns per 100 U.S. residents, the highest per capita in the world. In comparison, the second highest gun ownership per capita is Serbia, with 58 guns per 100 residents.

The debate regarding gun control extends beyond California and the United States. The United Nations has tried to create an international treaty to regulate global arms trades, which is estimated at $60 billion every year. The treaty would require all countries to establish national regulations to control the transfer of firearms and to regulate firearms brokers. Presently, there are 192 member States of the United Nations.

CHAPTER 7

GUN CONTROL EXPLAINED

They're trying to take away my guns! My rights shall not be infringed! Guns should be banned in America!

These are some of the default ideas people fall on when anyone talks about gun control – but propositions for gun control are usually neither as strict as either the gun-nuts or gun-phobics think they are.

The truth is that basically no countries in the world are completely gun-free – they're nearly always available at least available for hunters, farmers, the military, sports, or in other professional or non-lethal capacities.

When we talk about gun control we're talking about whether guns should be restricted specifically for regular civilian use, and usually in reference to personal defense. In reality in the USA we already have enough gun control when it comes to hunting, farming, and sport that the debate about gun control can only really be about self-defense.

In theory you might be able to use any gun you want to go hunting in America, but in reality unless you are shooting rats you will need a license to hunt big game (which requires you passing a training course), the kinds of guns you can use will be restricted unless you are on your private land (and if you're not a land baron that's unlikely), and there are already many restrictions in place in popular hunting locations such as not being able to use high capacity rifles for hunting.

Furthermore, people aren't that concerned about gun control regarding hunters or farmers. The debate is all about guns in the hands of accountants, bakers, and teachers when they are sat at home in their lounge rooms.

There are many different levels and types of gun control. At the extremes, you'll find complete blanket bans on guns of any type. On the other end, there would be almost no restrictions on the types of guns you could own, you'd be able to conceal carry them, no restrictions on who can get them, and you'd be legally justified in using them to defend yourself.

Very few people realistically believe there shouldn't be any gun or weapon control. Even the most strident gun believers would likely be uncomfortable knowing the lumber next door had a garage full of rocket launchers and weapon-grade drones.

So the question is about measures of gun control and how much we need. Currently, it varies from state to state regarding which kinds of guns you can get, how easily you can get them, and what you can do with them.

CHAPTER 8

GUNS CRIME IN THE USA

The rate of nearly all types of crime in the USA has been steadily declining for years and considering so much crime is done to criminals the chances of you facing violent crime is quite unlikely in most parts of the USA. Statistics for rates of victimization are essentially useless because they work on averages, but on average 18 men and 15 women out of 100,000 will face a violent crime each year in the USA. In other terms you have a 1 in 21,100 chance of being murdered in the USA.

To prevent that with a gun you would need to have the gun ready and on you. You would also most likely be shooting someone you know in your own home. The reality is that even if guns were proven to save you from crime you are very unlikely to need the protection.

When it comes down to it there is very little evidence that guns will effectively reduce crime overall or that you will need one. You are not a statistic though, and if you know you can safely handle a gun then perhaps it might save you – and ultimately that is what matters. Though carrying a gun for protection when you have no enemies and you are not in a high crime area is bordering delusional when looking at the statistics.

Gun control is one of the trickiest and most pressing issues in contemporary American politics. Unless you're blindly against or for gun control that is – in which case it's a simple and everyone else is just making it too complicated.

Why is it such a big issue though and what's so tricky about it?

There are the many reasons why so many people say gun control is an important issue.

In favor of gun control, people say that in a modern civilized society there is no reason for everyone and their grandmothers to own an assault rifle complete with detachable add-ons. Guns don't protect people, in fact, they are designed to kill people, and things like public massacres would be significantly reduced in number if guns were taken away.

Citizens against gun control say that guns are necessary to protect individuals from criminals, psychopaths, and an out-of-control government. The dangers of guns are grossly exaggerated, and the introduction of gun control is a red herring giving the already corrupt government permission to take away our rights slowly.

Those are the reasons people give, but the debate about gun control is bigger than that. Gun control is probably the biggest debate of the two prevailing ideologies of American politics that has come face to face in their purest forms.

On the one hand, you have the typical Republican or libertarian argument that government is not to be trusted and we need to be able to look after ourselves. On the other hand, you have the idea that things are better when done as a collective and government is capable of protecting and helping us.

Gun control is a question about what kind of a country America wants to be. One that has guns and is willing to use them given the chaotic nature of the world; or one that believes throwing them away can bring us closer to peace because change is possible. It's the classic conservative versus progressive argument.

So why is the argument so tricky?

Well, because most people have no idea what they are talking about and they're not willing, to be honest about the evidence that is there. Are other countries without guns better off? How often do people get killed with guns versus other weapons? Would we be safer or less safe without guns?

This is where this book comes in by helping you understand what gun control is; what it would mean for the USA to have more gun control, and examining the evidence from home and around the world for what it can tell us about the reality of having guns and gun control.

We'll start by looking at what gun control is and what we mean when we talk about guns and our constitutional rights. Then we'll try to assess what the reality currently is about guns, how often people shoot each other with them, and how hard it is to get them.

After that groundwork is done, we'll look around the world to see what gun control means in countries like Switzerland, Northern Ireland, or Sweden where guns are readily found, and in other countries like England, Australia, and Japan where guns are harder to find than above-ground diamonds.

We'll look at the common arguments for or against gun control and see whether they can be used to protect us or not.

Some of you will be wondering whether this book is for or against guns or gun control (you'll see soon there is a difference between the two). However, this book aims to improve the debate about guns and to make people better informed and more critical about their own opinions on the topic.

CHAPTER 9

SIX THINGS TO TEACH ABOUT SCHOOL RAMPAGE SHOOTINGS

Like a lot of people, I have gotten preoccupied with the dreadful news from Newtown, Connecticut. I have followed the news reports and reactions posted on social media. One suggested that school rampage shootings could be avoided if only teachers were taught to carry guns. I take umbrage at this "solution." Thankfully rampage shootings are rare enough not to justify it.

Because an elementary school was targeted I wonder what else can be done to reduce the probability of another occurrence. Fortunately, the U.S. Department of Education has researched school tragedies, and investigators have identified five contributing factors. Each of these five factors suggests things we can do as parents, educators and concerned citizens to head off yet another school tragedy.

1. Teach Acceptance

The first factor listed is the perception of being extremely marginalized. Peer relations for teenagers can get complicated. It is a tough time for them to deal with changes and the cliques that form. In tightly knit communities there is not the option to remain anonymous. Thus isolation usually leads to harassment, intimidation, and bullying. Our society at a time seems quite intolerant of differences. We need to teach cooperative activities that stress the importance of diversity in problem-solving.

2. Teach Resilience

The second factor listed is psychosocial problems. Understand that a person cannot help it if they have a mental illness such as depression, or an emotional disturbance. An abused person may not always show signs of their affliction. Some information suggests the shooter in Newton was a student with Asperger's (which incidentally is being dropped from DSM-5). While students with Autism spectrum disorder may have difficulty relating socially it does not mean they all have difficulty coping with their environment or that we should lower expectations. Failure can be therapeutic when overcome.

3. Teach Conflict Resolution Skills

A third factor given is a "cultural script." Rampage shooters are almost always male. Coincidence? Perhaps there is something written in man-code that says violent attacks will resolve problems and gain manly respect. We need to teach, and model for adolescents preferred behaviors and ways of standing up for oneself that does not involve violence.

4. Teach Confidentiality

A fourth factor is a failure of surveillance. Identification of a troubled teen must happen promptly. Adolescents are likely taught the opposite which is not to 'snitch' on your peers. This is particularly tricky since as mentioned above an afflicted student may not show signs of a problem. So if there is a possible threat a student must have confidence the adult they report it to will handle the information with care and ensure anonymity.

5. Keep Weapons Out of Schools

The last factor listed was gun availability. Shooting happens when the youngster obtains a lethal device. The overkill capability of weapons in this country is astounding. Unsupervised access to large caches of guns and ammunition is a problem. The extreme firing rate capability of (semi-) automatics with high count magazines or clips of exploding bullets is disturbing

6. Do Something Positive

There was no sixth factor included. But I would add the famous quote, "Evil prevails when good men do nothing." Do the opposite of violence. Go out of your way to say something kind. Teachers have been under attack as being paid too much, having summers off, etc. Show some empathy.

CHAPTER 10

TEACHERS AND GUNS IN SCHOOLS

Most people would throw a complete fit at the idea of their children learning in an environment controlled by firearms. There is however, some method to the idea. It can possibly deter anyone who is stupid enough to try and hurt kids in school, if someone manages to get into the school teachers won't have to wait for the police, and it can give families a sense of security.

A teacher's ability to carry a concealed firearm in school has a very good chance that it would deter anyone who would be heartless enough to come into a school and try to harm children. The shooting in Connecticut is what really started the whole issue on how safe our kids really are.

If someone like the man that killed those poor kids were to see on the news that a piece of legislature was passed allowing kids to carry weapons in school, he or she may just find the idea of trying to hurt kids in school impractical and useless. Just hearing that teachers can carry guns could keep the problem from ever occurring by causing the attacker to realize how much of a fool they were to think such a thing.

Another reason our teachers should be allowed to carry concealed weapons in schools is because if an intruder does manage to get into the school, the teachers will be prepared to handle the situation and won't have to wait an extended period of time. The police may have one or two officers stationed at the school, but if an intruder gets inside a classroom it's all up to the teacher to neutralize the situation.

Also, if there are no officers stationed at the school, who will be there to protect our kids if someone gets in? Teachers being allowed to carry concealed guns in school would bring reaction time to the situation to absolute zero.

The final reason that teachers should be allowed to carry concealed guns in school is because it can give our children and their families a sense of comfort that their kids are being considered and protected. If you were one of the families who lost a child in the Connecticut shooting, wouldn't you want the extra comfort knowing that your other children and their friends would be protected? Even though you went through so much and think nothing can help this can give you a little more hope knowing it will probably never happen again in your lifetime.

This comfort is available for you if you are willing to allow teachers to carry concealed firearms in school. Now, there is the liberal point of view to this. Guns are bad! Guns hurt people! I've got a bit of news for the liberals out there, but guns don't kill people. People with guns kill people. A gun can't pull its own trigger, only you can. People also say that it would be unsafe to have the teachers carrying the guns. They say, "What if the teacher is unstable?" One of the requirements in the process of receiving your concealed pistol license (CPL) is that you pass a background check. If a teachers background show any history of being unstable, they will be denied the ability to receive their CPL.

Those who are allowed to receive their CPL also have to pass a control test showing that they are able to handle a weapon. So in conclusion it would be a great opportunity to allow teachers to carry concealed weapons in school. It prevents bad situations from even occurring, it allows measures to be taken against the threat earlier, and it can bring a sense of calm to all of our families. So it's your choice and whether or not you are willing to trust the teachers your children interact with every day. How far are you willing to go to protect the lives of your children?

CHAPTER 11

WAYS THOUGHT TO MANAGE GUN SHOOTING IN SCHOOLS

The Problem with Zero Tolerance

Because of increasing incidents of school violence as well as school shootings, school district governing boards have adopted what is termed "zero tolerance" policies toward violent behavior, violent incidents, and any crime in general. Not tolerated would be infractions such as robbery, extortion, possession of drugs, weapons, assault, or causing serious injury to another. Violation of these rules could lead to expulsion when other means to fix the problem had failed, or the situation is such that there is a risk to others. While at first blush the concept would appear to be a good thing, its implementation has received mixed reviews. Opponents say that it enacts punishment, some say harsh punishment, for any violation of school rules without exceptions and any consideration of mitigating circumstances.

Paid Spies

Some school administrators should experiment with paying students for information about other students making threats and bringing drugs, alcohol, or weapons onto school grounds. It can be explained that in most of the well-publicized shootings the gunmen gave hints or said what they were planning to do.

Those in favor of paying will say that some kids won't come forward just because it's the right thing to do, but they will if there is a $50 payoff. In short, a money reward might encourage students to let someone know and possibly avert another tragedy. Students at one school felt that the program insulted their integrity because it assumed they needed payment to do the right thing.

Others thought it would lead to abuse by unscrupulous students filing false reports for the money. Still, others hope we can evolve to where we don't have to pay people. There are no figures as to its success or failure.

CHAPTER 12

LOCK-DOWN PROCEDURE AND RELATED INSURANCE

When school is in session, it was always given that our children were safe. Last week's FL gun massacre perpetrated by Nikolas Cruz where seventeen people were killed added to the uneasiness felt by parents across the nation.

No longer can we pretend that this type of violent tragedy cannot happen in any school across the United States.

It was in 2007 after all that alone gunman walked into the Blacksburg, VA Tech school and opened fire killing thirty-two innocents. And it was in 2012 that a man shot and killed thirty-two youngsters along with six teachers in the now infamous Sandy Hook Elementary School in Newtown, CT. Then in early September of 2016, a female student at the Alpine High in Brewster, TX shot and injured one student before committing suicide with the very same gun.

No wonder educational centers across the country take the recommended security procedures extremely seriously.

The lock-down procedure has been instituted as a safety procedure for every school, regardless of location. Just as the fire drill is standard, the school lock-down drill is conducted at two or three junctures throughout each year.

Below, the lock-down drill process is highlighted.

Each school usually follows comparable steps for student and staff member drills.

- Every door and exit-way is securely locked

- All students are evacuated into a designated safe zone in the center of the classroom; a spot that is not directly near a window or door

- The window blinds are drawn close.ed

- The class door window is shielded by a paper to stop an attacker from peeking insi.de

- Every light is turned off

- Each student and teacher keeps perfectly still in the safe classroom zone until school officials give the all-clear

Besides the three or four yearly lock-down drills, schools are advised to send literature depicting the lock-down procedure to all students and faculty, as well as to speak about the possibility so that the process is clear and understood in the event of an emergency.

Is there special insurance that protects from the financial loss and damages of an active shooter?

Just as there is terrorism insurance for the business owner, there is terrorism insurance that includes mass shooting liability coverage. This protects against lawsuits that accuse a school of alleged insufficient security, gun damage and counseling for the survivors of gun violence directed within the school premises and surrounding campus.

CHAPTER 13

WHAT YOU CAN DO- SCHOOL SHOOTINGS

When faced with a disaster or violent encounter, your first and best option is usually to run, not hide. Getting away from the threat is a priority. If you can safely remove yourself from the threat, your chances of survival are greatly increased.

The recent school shooting incidences demonstrated what happened to those individuals who didn't or couldn't get away from the threat. Tragically, some 9-11 victims had made it to safety before being told by officials to go back to their World Trade Center offices, only to perish when the buildings collapsed.

Korean survivors confirmed that passengers were repeatedly told to stay on board the doomed Sewol Ferry as the ship sank into the Yellow Sea. Many of the student passengers bundled themselves in life jackets, huddled in cubbies and followed the direction to "stay put." The video showing these children waiting for help that will never arrive is heartbreaking. Only later did we discover that the captain and many of the crew had already fled the ship.

Hiding and even barricading can be appropriate for certain active shooter or disaster situations, but when confronted, our kids need a survival plan. They need to know how to distance themselves from the threat safely. No matter how scary or uncomfortable, we owe our kids this information. Not discussing it or pretending it will never happen is not a strategy. They need to know all three options and that giving up is never acceptable.

All students need to become stakeholders in their safety and learn the run, hide and fight options and how to apply them when facing a violent encounter.

It's their right to know, and it may save their life. It's up to us to ensure they get the training they need.

CHAPTER 14

MY INDEPENDENT THOUGHT ON GUNS IN SCHOOLS

It's been years since Sandy Hook. Still, nothing has been done. There was another one in Colorado, then recently Marjory Stoneman Douglas High School in Parkland, Florida. When is it going to happen? What are we waiting for? We need a law. It's simple... one law. No one can shoot a weapon and murder someone at a school. I know we have no murder as a law. I know we have no weapons at school as a law. No law affirms that you cannot shoot someone on school property. This is the loophole. This is why it keeps happening. Boom we're done. Problem solved.

Obviously, it's not that simple. I wish it were. I wish we could make laws and laws would protect us from bad things happening. Unfortunately, sometimes the presence of laws can be more dangerous than the absence of laws. I'll give you an example. What if we've made a law that makes it illegal for a shark to attack you or for a jellyfish to sting you. Well, if you believed me then you would swim with no fear. You wouldn't worry about that jellyfish because it can't attack you... it's illegal.

Now, people would look at me like I'm crazy. They would say, "No law can protect you from a wild animal." Exactly. No law can ever protect us. In fact, laws should only be in place for retribution. So, if someone does something bad to you, we have grounds for a measure of revenge for the wrong that they've done. We have created a "gun-free zone." Schools are a killing zone for the wildest animals on earth. The equivalent would be dropping you into the middle of the ocean with a sign, "No sharks allowed" on your back. We aren't dealing with humans; we're dealing with predators.

In all honesty, I think it would be great to live in a world with no guns. I use guns for hunting. I use guns for protection. If I had the chance to exist in a world where a gun was never made I would be OK with that. Now, back to reality... that's never going to happen. The truth is guns are all around us. Do you realize how many times you've been at a mall and the person sitting next to you at the food court has a concealed weapon? Do you ever think about the person driving in front of you having a handgun underneath the seat?

Will allowing people to have guns on school property stop school shootings altogether? No. Laws don't work. We don't tell someone they are completely safe in the ocean. We warn them of the danger that lurks out there and tells them to swim at their own risk. Guess what, life is live at your own risk. Wish you could protect good people from bad things happening. If you made a law tomorrow that made all guns illegal, does anybody think that people wouldn't still have guns? No. I truly believe gun control people are trying to do what's best for the kids. Unfortunately, all laws do is hurt people who abide by them. Good, upstanding people would give you the guns because they don't want to break the law. Predators would keep their guns and be glad that no one is there to fight against them.

My hope though is that in school shootings we remember that there are people involved. A school shooting is not a time for a crusade either way. Real people do get hurt by guns. Making a new law tomorrow is not going to prevent it from ever happening again. The battle should never be about guns. The battle should be between the 99% people who have respect for human life vs. the 1% predator who devours innocence.

CONCLUSION

We have heard the very sad stories about high school students who have gone on rampages and killed students and teachers at their schools. We have also heard stories about abusive relationships that have gone bad and guns have been used. These stories have been very heartbreaking and sad, but there are stories in the news that are even sadder than this.

Those stories are those that have been accidental, and it has been with family or close friends. There have been the stories of children getting into the closet or cupboard and finding a gun. They play with it, and it goes off, and a friend or family member is accidentally killed. There have even been hunting stories or other stories of not putting the lock on the guns correctly or not unloading the guns correctly. These stories are very heartbreaking and can cause people to be scared to even be around guns.

The important thing to remember is that there are the other stories where having a gun license and having a gun in their possession has been a positive thing. The important thing to remember is that there are safety precautions that have to be taken. One of the things that people can do not to be afraid of guns is to take gun safety classes. With the safety classes, people will learn several different things to help protect their family and themselves. It is important to recognize that in many states a gun license is required to purchase or handle guns, and on top of that, gun safety classes are required to get the gun license. But with licensing and proper training in place, guns can be a good thing.

Thank You once again for downloading this book.

I hope you enjoyed it. Please kindly leave for a review for others to know how you feel about this book.

Please check out my twitter fan page at:
twitter.com/cbashsuperdome

Also like my Facebook fan page and look out for new books:
facebook.com/wisebookz

www.ingramcontent.com/pod-product-compliance
Lightning Source LLC
Chambersburg PA
CBHW070406230526
45471CB00006B/2685